A MIND AT EASE

A MIND AT EASE

By

MARION L. ASHTON, M.B., Ch.B.

published by

(part of Overcomer Literature Trust Ltd.)

10 MARLBOROUGH ROAD, PARKSTONE,
POOLE, DORSET BH14 OHJ, ENGLAND

1st Edition: October, 1961
2nd Edition: April, 1963
3rd Edition: September, 1964
4th Edition: October, 1966
5th Edition: January, 1968
6th Edition: August, 1969
7th Edition: August, 1971
8th Edition: August, 1973
9th Edition: August, 1976
10th Edition: November, 1979
11th Edition: October, 1984

ISBN 0 947788 25 5

Printed in Great Britain by Gospel Press, South Molton, Devon.

CONTENTS

A mind at ease is life and health

Proverbs 14:30 (Moffatt)

INTRODUCTION

OF recent years the words ' tension ' and ' stress ' have been increasingly used in medicine.

Doctors speak of mental, nervous, or emotional tension, and of stress-symptoms, stress-behaviour, or stress, changes. At Medical Conferences they have discussed the Meaning, the Causes, and the Treatment of tension and stress, and have expressed deep concern over the great increases in the use of tranquillising drugs for these states.

The Bible gives us promises concerning " perfect peace ", " peace that passeth understanding ", " rest ", " a mind at ease ", all of which awake in the hearts of many, a cry that they might be helped to find the way of passing from *stress* to *rest*.

My aim, in writing what follows, is to share in the simplest possible language, some of the things concerning this subject, which I have learned as a doctor, some from my study of the Bible, some from the experience of others, and some from personal experience, as I have sought to deal with areas in my own personality which I have known to be subject to tension.

CHAPTER I

THE MEANING AND RESULTS OF TENSION

SOME degree of tension is normal to the human frame. The athlete's muscles are in a state of tension while running in a race, the student's mind is in a state of tension while he is studying or doing an examination. We are often brought into states of emotional tension through sorrow or joy, or through the strain of entering into the problems and sufferings of others. This sort of tension is the normal response of our bodies to the demands made upon us, and does us no harm, in fact it only increases our capacity to act or think or feel. Normal tension is always followed by relaxation. When the race is over the muscles relax, when the examination is over the brain relaxes, when the emotional strain ends there is relaxation. If the muscles refused to relax the normal state of tension would pass into one which is abnormal. If the brain of the student refused to relax the normal would pass into an abnormal mental tension. If the emotions refused to relax the normal tension would pass into abnormal emotional tension. It is this abnormal persistent tension which is meant when doctors speak of mental and emotional tension.

Sometimes the tension is abnormally prolonged so that the person concerned never relaxes mentally or emotionally, at other times the tension is far greater than is justified by the circumstances. The person who is in a state of mental tension will turn every " mole-hill into a mountain ", the one who is in a state of emotional tension will weep at every small mishap.

These abnormal tensions sooner or later produce results and lead to what are known as stress-symptoms or stress-behaviour. The nature of the results varies according to the personality of the one affected, but in every case it has the opposite effect to that of normal tension, it decreases the ability to act and think and feel normally.

The results of tension may range from the minor reactions which all of us must recognise and suffer from at times, to serious physical and mental illness.

Owing to the fact that the mental and physical is so closely related in our make-up, it is impossible to draw a clear line between results which are mental and nervous, and those which are physical; however, for the sake of clarity it may be helpful to divide the results into those which are primarily mental or nervous, and those which are primarily physical.

Results of tension which are primarily mental include insomnia, lack of concentration, a mind which " goes round in circles ", different forms of hysteria, anxiety states in which the patient is always anxious and apprehensive quite apart from circumstances, and chronic depression.

The simplest physical symptoms resulting from tension are those which we all know only too well because they can be passing accompaniments of normal tension. We know the loss of appetite and insomnia associated with anxiety, the palpitations which accompany fear, and amongst students there is a condition known as " examination diarrhoea ". Normally these all pass away when the strain passes, but in conditions of stress they may continue persistently. Dr. Paul Adolph, in his helpful book, HEALTH SHALL SPRING FORTH, writes concerning these physical symptoms, " Three of the more common tension patterns suggest themselves for mention which for convenience we may name:

(1) The stiff-neck pattern; (2) the chest tension pattern; and (3) the stomach tension pattern." Later he writes, " These patterns may co-exist or may change from one to the other."[1]

An experienced doctor learns to recognise one of these three patterns in a patient and will quickly realise that the underlying cause is tension.

In the first, the patient complains of a stiff or painful neck, the pain often ru `ng up the back of the head, and giving the patient a feeling of constriction in the head, or of a tight band around the head.   This is often associated with difficulty in sleeping.

The second set of symptoms focus upon the heart and the patient is often convinced that there is real heart trouble.   Palpitations and feelings of constriction and pressure round `he heart are the commonest of the symptoms in this ,roup.

The stomach tension may show itself in feelings of nausea or of continual feelings of fulness, so that the appetite is impaired.

It is interesting to notice that expressions which we commonly use, show that there is recognition of the fact that these symptoms can be caused by mental reactions. We speak of a person as being " a pain in the neck ! " We say we must get things " off our chests ", and how many times have we said that we are " sick " of a thing or that we are " fed up ! "

Then there is a group of illnesses in which the primary cause may be tension, these include asthma, rheumatoid arthritis, and certain skin rashes.

In some cases of stomach ulcer, and of an inflammation

of the lower bowel known as mucous colitis the chief cause is tension.

Quite apart from being the primary cause of certain sicknesses, it is well known in the medical profession that tension tends to lower resistance to disease, and to increase the severity and length of any illness.

Even if the tension is not serious enough to cause any of these symptoms or illnesses, we know that the smallest degree of abnormal tension hinders the one who suffers from it from being his best physically and mentally. For those who are Christians, therefore, it is of great importance to recognise tension in its early stages, and seek to find the way of rest and release. Our whole beings have been bought by the Lord Jesus Christ to become temples of the living God, and to be used in His Service, we should desire therefore that our minds and bodies be efficient, and that we avoid, if possible, states of tension.

I have spoken of mental and physical results of tension but there are also spiritual results. Tension robs us of that rest and quietness of heart which is so essential to close communion with God. God says to us, "Be still and know that I am God," but stillness is impossible to the one whose mind and emotions are in a state of tension. Our fellowship with God and our knowledge of God are hindered by tension.

Our witness to the Lord Jesus and our usefulness in His service are marred by tension. Unbelievers are very quick to discern whether Christians have minds at ease and are really resting in the Lord; they are not likely to listen seriously to such invitations as that of the Lord Jesus when He said, " Come unto Me and I will give you rest," if the invitation is passed on to them by those who, though professing to know the Lord, are not displaying in their lives the rest which He gives. There are many people in these days who are subjects of great tension, anxiety and fear are gnawing at their hearts and minds, and they long for someone to help them.   They are not likely to be drawn to the Christian who is in a state of tension, but they will be drawn in their troubles to one who is truly manifesting the rest and peace of the Lord and who has " a heart at leisure from itself, to soothe and sympathise ".

Our relationship with fellow-Christians is marred by tension.   A Christian in a state of tension is likely to be irritable, and easily upset; misunderstanding and strained relationships may follow and hinder that fellowship of the Spirit which is such a blessing in any work for the Lord.

As we think of these things we may well echo the prayer of the hymn-writer:

> " Take from our lives the strain and stress,
> And let our ordered lives confess
> The beauty of Thy Peace."

Reference:
(1)   HEALTH SHALL SPRING FORWARD, pp. 15 and 17.

CHAPTER 2

THE CAUSES OF TENSION

AS we consider the causes of tension we must first question whether the causes are inside the person concerned or outside. That is, is mental tension due to the strains and stresses of modern life, or is it due to something within the personality of the one who is suffering from tension? The answer to that question is that mental tension is caused by some sort of conflict within the personality of the one concerned. Outside circumstances may precipitate symptoms of mental tension and expose it, but they are not the primary cause.

We realise the truth of this as we consider the lives of people we know or read about. We must all have seen people go through fiery trials and yet remain in peace and mental equilibrium. We know of those who have been in solitary confinement and yet have not suffered from mental tension, though, of course, they have suffered mentally as well as physically.

Paul, when going through experiences of great strain, wrote, " We are handicapped on all sides, but we are never frustrated; we are puzzled, but never in despair," 2 Corinthians 4: 8 (Phillips' translation) and writing from prison, chained to his guard, he bore witness that he had learned in whatever state he was, to be content. He also spoke of " fightings without and fears within " 2 Corinthians 7: 5. He certainly knew " a mind at ease " in spite of his distressing circumstances.

On the other hand we must all have seen people who show signs of suffering from mental tension when their circumstances are far less trying than those mentioned above.

The following are quotations from medical experts on this subject:

" It isn't what happens to a person that matters, so much as how he *reacts* to what happens to him, and how he reacts will be determined by his inner resources of heart and mind—his fundamental philosophy, his innermost religion and what he really believes."[1]

" Stress is popularly referred to as if it were exogenous (from without) as, for example, in the phrase ' the pressures of modern life '. This is a mistake. It is largely endogenous (from within). It is not so much the fierce situation, but the individual's reaction to it, which determines the effects of stress. . . . Often the stressed person is found to be agitated about no real cause. He has made his ' stress ' for himself."[2]

" Conflict is now generally recognised as the main basis of neurosis."[3]

We need to be very clear on this point, for it is one which we often instinctively resist, and it is very important when we come to consider the prevention or cure of tension. Many people who are suffering from tension like to feel that it is due to the very difficult circumstances in which they have been placed, and think that if only they could change their circumstances they would recover. They are very reluctant to admit that the primary cause is within their own personalities. Yet in this very fact lies their greatest hope. We who are Christians have not been promised easy circumstances. The Lord Jesus said, " In the world ye shall have tribulation " (John 16: 33). Peter spoke of the fiery trial which was to try those to whom he wrote (1 Peter 4: 12).   Paul, writing to Timothy, told him that in the last days there will come times of stress (2 Timothy 3: 1, R.S.V.).   If a mind at ease depends on our circumstances, then we must all face the fact that we may be plunged into circumstances too difficult for us to bear, and if we seek peace of mind by trying to run away from those circumstances, we are quite likely to run into some even more difficult.   To a large extent we are unable to control the circumstances and pressures which come into our lives.

While we have not been promised easy circumstances, we have been given a mighty Saviour Who knows us completely and Who is able to save to the uttermost those that come to God by Him (Hebrews 7: 25).   He said, " Learn of Me and ye shall find rest unto your souls " (Matthew 11: 29).   When He spoke of tribulation He also said, " These things have I spoken unto you, that in Me ye might have peace " (John 16: 33).   If we admit that the cause of our tension is within ourselves, we can at the same time place ourselves into the hands of the Great Physician, Who can search into the very depths of our beings and straighten out the underlying conflicts, and speak His peace to our souls.   The Lord Jesus Himself said that a kingdom divided against itself cannot stand; we all know that a kingdom in which there is conflict will not be able to stand up against an enemy, and on the contrary we know the truth of the saying " unity is strength ".   This is true of our personalities.   The personality in which there is conflict is much more likely to give way under the pressure of difficult circumstances, than the one which is integrated and truly made whole by the Lord Jesus Christ.

If the cause of tension is some sort of conflict within the one concerned, we must go on to consider the causes of conflict within a personality.   I think we can divide these into two groups, namely, causes which are created in childhood, and those which arise in adult life.

In the first group are all the conflicts which arise from insecurity in early childhood. This is a very important group, in fact it has been said that " it must be realised that most mental illness (major and minor) is the direct outcome of unresolved conflict in early childhood."[4] One of the difficulties which arise from this cause is that the conflict is deep-seated and has often been driven down below the conscious levels of the mind, into what is called the subconscious, so that it cannot easily be remembered.

Every child needs security and love, and in many cases, where these are lacking, conflict is produced which sows the seeds of future mental and emotional tension.

Secondly, what are the causes which arise in adult life? In some ways these are simpler and easier to discover than those which have been created in childhood. Anything which produces conflict in a person may lead on to mental tension. Bishop Stephen Neill enumerates Fear, Frustration and Resentment as the three great enemies of man,[5] and it seems possible that all the causes of conflict could be included under one or other of these headings.

It would be impossible to enumerate all the causes and types of fear which assail the human personality. In Genesis 3: 10 we read the first recorded words of fallen man, and in the centre of those words is the statement " I was afraid ". Ever since then fear has dogged the human race, and there is no living human being who does not know fear in many varieties and forms. Fear may vary greatly in degree, it may be simply a protective instinct which is good and useful, or it may become terror and grip a person in such a way that he is quite paralysed. It may become like an obsession which is always present, eating away at the personality of the one concerned, and even if

forced into the background, is always ready to spring out
and take possession of the mind.   It is these last two which
cause mental tension.   I think it must be recognised that
there are some people who are more liable to fear than
others, certain temperaments are more given to be fearful,
and people in whom imagination is highly developed are
more subject to fear. Christians who know themselves to be
more subject temperamentally and mentally to fear than
some others will learn to ignore and even laugh at some of
their fears, but they will, with the Lord's help, not allow
their fears to get a grip of them or become an obsession.

There are fears for which we know a reason, such as the
fear of what people think and say, fear of failure, fear of
sickness, particularly cancer, fear of old age and death,
and innumerable others.   There is fear which projects
itself into the future in the form of anxiety and worry, fear
which cannot get rid of the past and takes the form of
feelings of guilt.   There are fears which are based on
untruths, as in the case of a young woman who, because
she had had a major operation, was obsessed with the fear
of early death, and she needed to understand that she was
no more likely to die young than any other woman.

Then there are a host of fears which appear quite
unreasonable.   Sudden fear grips the personality without
there being any known cause for fear.   In these cases the
cause is very commonly one which goes right back into
childhood and has been pushed out of mind so that it is not
remembered.

Frustration may focus upon oneself, upon others, or
upon circumstances.   Frustration with oneself may take
the form of an inferiority complex, or of expecting far too
much of oneself, or of trying to do things for which one
is quite unfitted, and then getting disappointed and
depressed when one fails.

Frustration with others includes all the conflicts which are produced through difficulties in relationships with others. It may arise from an inability to accept others as they are. A wife may have a mental picture of what she would like her husband to be, often based upon an exaggerated idea of her own father, and because he does not fit in with that picture she is disappointed and frustrated. A father may have a deep desire for a son to follow in his profession, and may not be able to accept that the boy has none of the qualities to fit him for that particular profession, his frustration and disappointment may make him quite unable to accept other good qualities in his son.

Some sort of frustration because of circumstances is so common that most people accept it as inevitable and do not realise the harm it can do to the personality, if it becomes a part of the mental outlook. Frustration with circumstances can be so great that the one concerned becomes quite unwilling to face the ordinary circumstances of everyday life, and it may then reveal itself in some illness which is just a form of escapism.

Resentment is perhaps the bitterest enemy of the personality and is well-described in Hebrews 12: 15 as a root of bitterness which troubles the person who has it and defiles many others. There are those who are suffering from mental tension because some resentment has been clung to for years. Perhaps it is resentment against parents or resentment against some friend, or even resentment against God for allowing some sorrow to come into the life. I have known a woman's whole life embittered and strained because she lost a child, and years afterwards she had not got rid of her resentment towards God. We who are Christians also need to remember that not only resentment but any hidden, unconfessed sin may be the cause of conflict leading on to mental tension.

There is another group of causes of some of the *symptoms* of mental and emotional tension which need to be considered, namely those which come from physical conditions. Insomnia may be a symptom of mental tension or it may be an accompaniment of some purely physical condition of ill-health. Depression may follow such illnesses as influenza or may accompany other chronic illnesses. In the tropics amoebic dysentery is almost always accompanied by depression, sometimes of a severe nature. Emotional instability frequently accompanies certain conditions in women, such as pregnancy and the " change of life ". I have found that people suffering in these ways often think they are suffering from real mental tension when they are not. They say they are " neurotic " or "going mental", and just to explain to them that their symptoms have a definite physical basis is a help and comfort.

Added to these causes of tension some people have inherited tendencies and inherent weaknesses over which they have no natural control. Again, the important thing for a Christian is to come to an understanding of himself so that he is not condemning himself for something in which he is not to blame. I have met tenderhearted, sensitive Christians who would be brought into a place of great liberty if they would stop condemning themselves for certain things for which they are not responsible; I have also met Christians of many years standing whose lives would be transformed if they would start to condemn, amongst other things, bitterness, resentment, outbursts of temper, frustrations such as are inexcusable, even if understandable, to one who is seeking to obey New Testament teaching. We need, on this point, the illumination of the Holy Spirit and sometimes the help of others to enable us to understand the truth about ourselves.

In thinking of the causes of tension, I would like to add a few thoughts concerning the part played by our great enemy Satan, in these conditions. Many Christians tend to go to one of two extremes; either they ignore altogether the fact that Satan's chief battleground is the mind, and that he is intensely interested in provoking and using conditions of mental tension, or else they make so much of Satan and evil spirits that they fail to recognise that there may be natural causes which need to be brought to the light and understood if the sufferer is to be healed. Both these extremes are wrong and we need the discernment of the Holy Spirit that we may neither ignore Satan nor overestimate or wrongly estimate his activities.

Of course Satan is behind all the sin and sorrow and conflict in human life, but we need to remember that he would have no power over man had man not given him a door of entry by disobedience to God. I think his part is pre-eminently one of taking advantage of the weaknesses of our natures and using them as a vantage ground from which he can work.

Satan is the father of lies (John 8: 44), and probably the biggest contribution he makes towards the causation of mental tension is by presenting lies to the minds of God's children; lies about themselves, lies about other people, lies about God Himself. Not only does he lie but he seeks always to cover the truth and keep hidden the real source of a person's trouble.

Satan is also the accuser of the brethren (Revelation 12: 10) and almost invariably Christian people, who are suffering from any sort of mental tension or even the nervous symptoms caused by physical illness, have their sufferings increased by the accusations of Satan. Frequently I have talked with those who are suffering from depression and found that their depression is being increased by Satan telling them that the cause of their trouble is spiritual, when in fact it is not, and so they go down from depression to self-condemnation, and often despair. Satan sometimes finds allies in well-meaning Christian friends, who take this same line and so increase the condemnation of the sufferer. On the other hand Satan sometimes hides up the fact that a person's primary trouble is spiritual, and then the one concerned starts on an endless round of consultations with doctors and even psychiatrists, not realising a straight talk with a discerning friend could show him the way out of his difficulties.

I believe, too, that Satan has a great deal to do with the fear that is based on vague feelings of guilt.

References:

[1]   IN THE SERVICE OF MEDICINE. I.V.F. Jan., 59. Religion and Nervous Breakdown by Arthur Pool, M.B., Ch.B., M.R.C.P., D.P.M. Consultant Psychiatrist, Oldham and Rochdale Hospital Group.

[2]   IN THE SERVICE OF MEDICINE. I.V.F. July 59. What do we mean medically by 'Stress'? Notes from a discussion introduced by Douglas Mac G. Jackson, M.D., F.R.C.S., and Duncan Vere, M.D., M.R.C.P.

[3]   A CHRISTIAN APPROACH TO PSYCHOLOGICAL MEDICINE. I.V.F. p. 16.

[4]   A CHRISTIAN APPROACH TO PSYCHOLOGICAL MEDICINE. I.V.F., p. 23.

[5]   A GENUINELY HUMAN EXISTENCE. Stephen Neill. p. 190.

CHAPTER 3

THE PREVENTION OF TENSION

AS we have considered the causes of mental tension we must realise that we all have within us the seeds of tension. There is not one of us who would claim to be completely free at all times from any sort of inner conflict. We also know that doctors are treating an ever-increasing number of patients whose primary trouble is mental and nervous rather than physical. In view of these things it should become a serious question with each one of us as to how we can prevent ourselves from getting into states of real mental tension. None of us can afford to treat the question lightly.

Let us then think of some of the things which will help us in the prevention of mental tension.

First and foremost we need to have a clear understanding and conviction that it is God's will, as revealed in the Bible, that His children should enjoy real peace and rest of heart and mind, even in the midst of tribulation. In 2 Timothy 1 : 7 we read, " God hath not given us the spirit of fear; but of power, and of love, and of a sound mind." In His infinite wisdom He does allow some of His children to go through times of nervous and mental suffering, even as He allows times of physical sickness, and in many of these cases the sufferer comes through the trial into a deeper peace than was known before, with more sympathy for others and with an ability to help others. At the same time we can be assured that God's Will and God's power are on the side of mental health and stability, and that every step we take in seeking to deal with the conflicts in our personalities is in the line of His Will for us. This conviction should be accompanied by a definite purpose that we shall allow God to deal drastically with any of the causes of conflict in our lives, so that increasing peace of mind will be our portion, and not increasing tension.

The prevention of tension also depends on our whole attitude to the Christian life. In these days there is much superficial and light thinking and living amongst Christians, and we need to remember that the Christian life is a battleground, not a playground. We live in days when it seems as if Satan's forces are being let loose as never before, when Christians are subjected to peculiar stresses and strains, and when in particular there seems an attack on the mental stability of God's children. We dare not play with these things, we must heed Peter's warning: " Be sober, be vigilant; because your adversary the devil, as a roaring lion, walketh about, seeking whom he may devour " (1 Peter 5: 8). In particular we should recognise those things which are the enemies of the human personality, and treat them as enemies, not just as unfortunate weaknesses, which are an inevitable part of life.

Let us think again of those three great enemies, fear, frustration and resentment, and realise that we must face them and deal with them *as soon as we are conscious of their presence*, rather than allow them to do their work in our personalities and bring about a state of mental tension. Perhaps the best way to deal with them is to think of the three great Christian qualities named by Paul in 1 Corinthians 13: 13, FAITH, HOPE, and LOVE. These are certainly the greatest friends of the human personality, and we can easily see that these are the qualities which will undo the work of the enemies, as we allow the Holy Spirit to bring them into our lives. (Let us remember that when the Bible speaks of hope, there is nothing vague about it,

as in our phrase " I hope so ", it is always a glad certainty.
For an example see Hebrews 6: 18-20.)

While Faith, Hope and Love are needed to expel fear,
the Bible is, in particular, full of instances of Faith expel-
ling Fear. If we turn to Psalm 46 we read: " God is our
refuge and strength, a very present help in trouble.
Therefore will not we fear, though the earth be removed,
and though the mountains be carried into the midst of the
sea; though the waters thereof roar and be troubled,
though the mountains shake with the swelling thereof."
In Psalm 56: 3 we hear the Psalmist say, " What time I
am afraid I will trust in Thee," and then in the next verse,
" in God I have put my trust; I will not fear ". We hear
the rebuke of the Lord Jesus to His disciples when they
were afraid of the storm at sea: " Why are ye fearful, O ye
of little faith ? " (Matthew 8: 26), and His Word of
encouragement to Jairus: " Be not afraid, only believe "
(Mark 5: 36).

At the same time as believing firmly that Faith is the
answer to all our fears, I do not believe that the pathway
of faith is always an easy one, or that it is possible glibly to
say, " Just trust the Lord and your fears will go ". I have
found that faith often has to wrestle before it rests. Faith
may have to lay hold of the Lord with great cryings and
tears, that He will reveal the basic cause of fear; faith may
have to cast itself in utter helplessness upon the Lord and
continue in prayer and seeking His face for a prolonged
period of time, before it is rewarded and fear cast out.
Real faith is willing for this pathway and will find in
experience the way of diligently seeking Him, until the
glad day dawns when it can sing with the Psalmist, " I
sought the Lord and He heard me and delivered me from
all my fears " (Psalm 34: 4).

I would like here to quote from a letter recently received: " I had a very wonderful experience over the week-end. You know something of my fears and inadequacy where illness is concerned ! Nobody knows just how much the fear has dogged me, and I've never really faced it because I've never been in a situation where I've had to. But the climax was reached on Saturday when I was left alone with B . . . still in bed and her mother very ill ! I knew I'd got to cope entirely alone until Sunday night, when Sister said she would phone, and come for the night if Saturday had been bad. I'd already had bad nights and days of fearful apprehension and fear, and wasn't feeling well because I'd had a terrific fluey cold. I sat in an armchair for a few minutes in *complete* despair. I was saying to myself, ' This is it—you've got to face it now, and you can't ', and I was desperately thinking of *any* way to get out of it. Then in utter desperation I said to God something like this, ' If You are all that You claim to be You can deal with this, and if You can't, then nothing about You is true—it's all or nothing. Prove to me that You are sufficient for this.' Then I went to get some food for B . . . , and while I was busy in the kitchen I suddenly realised that my stomach was no longer in knots and the apprehension had gone. During the day and night there were times when I thought it would sweep over me again, but each time I reminded God that He had said He was sufficient, and peace came again. I was awake all night with Mrs. M . . . , but knew no fear or anxiety or apprehension. That peace has stayed with me, and the biggest fear in my life which started as far as I can remember on the Sunday night that my father had his haemorrhage, has gone. Of course, it's been a completely irrational fear—I've always known that, but it's been a crippling burden, and has made me a terrible coward and willing to resort to anything rather than have to cope with sickness. It's got even to this extent, that if anyone came to see me at work and looked ill, or said they felt ill, I couldn't concentrate on helping them but got rid of them as soon as possible. I hadn't been able to prepare anything for Class, and Sister was here so that I could go. Until the hymn before the talk I had no idea what to say—then I spoke on, ' I love the Lord, because He hath heard the voice of my supplication,' and I talked about how God can cope with the hidden fears of our hearts. I've decided that quite definitely it's true that though we believe not, yet He abideth faithful ! I had no faith in His power to cope with me. I only knew He was my only hope ! . . . It's impossible to express the wonder of such an experience because I could never express the strength of the irrational fear."

This letter is from a middle-aged lady who could not be considered to be in a real state of mental tension from her hidden fear, but she easily could have been, and it had caused her to be quite incapable of helping anyone who was sick. There are several things illustrated by this letter; the origin of the fear (her father died, following the hæmorrhage mentioned, when she was just sixteen years old), the unreasonableness of the fear, the fact that it had to be faced to be overcome, and God's power to remove it. Another very interesting thing is that the one concerned did not realise that from her side Fear was being removed by Faith. She says, " I had no faith in His power to cope with me—I only knew He was my only hope ! " Of course that *is* Faith, though many people do not recognise it as such. It is *Faith* that casts itself upon God as the only hope. That *is* the kind of Faith which casts out Fear.

What about Frustration ? Surely frustration with myself is counteracted by Faith and Hope. Hope which gives a certain assurance that God has a specific plan and purpose for my life, and that He will fulfil that plan. Hope which tells me that God has a work for me to do which none other can do, a place to fill which none other can fill. Faith which believes that God has put into me the very qualities necessary to fulfil His purpose without seeking to do things which are beyond me and outside His purpose.

Frustration with others is counteracted by faith, hope and love. Love which is willing to accept the other as he really is, with all his faults and failings, faith which trusts God to work out His purpose in him, and hope which sees him, not as he is now but as God will make him.

Frustration with circumstances is expelled only by real faith in the sovereignty of God and by love which is willing to submit to His Will. Faith in the fact that *all* things are working together for good to those that love God. A faith that admits no second causes but which accepts every circumstance as being allowed by Him. A faith which recognises that even if Satan brings something into the life, it has only come because God has allowed it for a purpose, as in the case of Job and of Paul (2 Corinthians 12: 7-10).

There is one kind of frustration which is so common that it needs to be given a place on its own; it is the frustration which occurs in the realm of sex impulses. There are many voices today which are encouraging young people to think that all restraint in this realm is frustration, and is therefore harmful. This is a lie, and is doing untold harm. There is far more real frustration in the wrong use of the sex impulse than in its restraint. A Christian young man may yearn for a deep friendship with a Christian girl, and may not find much encouragement. He may wonder whether he can ever win the girl he loves without compromising with the world's lack of moral standards. The teaching of Scripture may appear un-realistic in the face of contemporary attitudes to sex, but the Lord makes His Will come to pass for those who commit every step to His Loving Care. " He faileth not " (Zephaniah 3: 5), and we should always remember that " He leadeth us in the paths of *righteousness* for His Name's sake " (Psalm 23: 3). There must be many young people suffering from various degrees of conflict because of the real guilt attached to hidden immoral relationships. On the other hand, we all know many unmarried Christian men and women who are healthy in body and balanced in mind, living useful, unfrustrated lives, and who give every evi-dence of being truly satisfied in the Lord and in their work.

Unmarried women often go through difficult times, when their hearts cry out for the satisfaction of married life and the joy of having children of their own. I have seen Christian women come triumphantly through such times, and I have seen others develop such a sense of frustration that the symptoms of mental tension appear in their lives. Though each one has to battle through this question on her own, I believe there are secrets of victory and of the prevention of tension, in our three friends, Faith, Hope and Love, and in the knowledge of the truth. Let me briefly state what I believe to be these secrets.

The truth is that married life (satisfying as it is when in the Lord), and having children (wonderful as that is), do not satisfy the deepest needs of the human heart. We have all met married people who are obviously unsatisfied, and we have also met unmarried people who are deeply satisfied. We need to know the truth that the Lord Jesus Christ, and He alone, can satisfy the deepest needs of the human heart; no one else can; nothing else can. We also need to know with glad certainty that He can and does satisfy. " He satisfieth the longing soul and filleth the hungry soul with goodness " (Psalm 107: 9). " Thou openest Thy hand, and satisfiest the desire of every living thing " (Psalm 145: 16).

Another secret is the Faith which believes that God has a specific plan for each life as regards marriage, and that His plan is best; and the hope which gives the assurance that He will bring about His plan, and will undertake for everything that is involved in that plan, whether it be a married life or an unmarried life.

The last secret is Love; real self-sacrificing Love which gives out to others. This sort of Love is not only a blessing to others but wonderfully satisfying to the heart. The unmarried person who seeks to replace the particular love of marriage by an exclusive friendship or possessive affection, will remain frustrated and unsatisfied. The one who seeks to pour out Love for the Lord Himself, and then for others in sacrificial service, will be satisfied and fulfilled.

If we are ever to deal with resentment, that bitter enemy, we must have Love, for in Love is mercy and a forgiving spirit. The Love about which Paul speaks always has an element of self-sacrifice, it is forgetful of injuries done to it, whereas resentment is essentially self-centred, and full of self-pity. For one who finds it hard to give up resentment, a good passage of Scripture to read and meditate upon prayerfully is Matthew 18: 23-35.

If Fear, Frustration and Resentment are often based on lies, and aggravated by lies, Faith, Hope and Love are based on Truth, and so the Christian who would be kept from mental tension should be extremely interested in the discernment of truth. We need to know the truth about ourselves, the truth about others, the truth concerning the cause of our conflicts. The Psalmist said, " Thou desirest truth in the inward parts " (Psalm 51: 6). Jesus said,

" Ye shall know the truth and the truth shall set you free " (John 8: 32). We have been given the Word of Truth, the Spirit of Truth, and a Saviour Who said, " I am the Truth." As we meditate constantly in the Word, as we submit our minds and whole personalities to the Spirit, and as we share the very life of our Saviour, we shall be increasingly sensitive to the truth, and increasingly able to discern what is not according to Truth.

Very close to truth is sincerity. Shakespeare said, " To thine own self be true, and it must follow as the night the day, thou canst not then be false to any man." The beginning of conflict in some people is a lack of sincerity which is not true to itself. If we would avoid tension let us be true to our own selves, which means acting according to that which we really believe. It is so easy to act according to what people think we ought to believe rather than what we do believe. Insincerity causes conflict because it does violation to our real selves.

Since any hidden sin can be the cause of conflict, it is essential that we walk in the light with God, sensitive to sin, and ready quickly to confess and forsake any known sin. " He that hideth his sins shall not prosper: but whoso confesseth and forsaketh them shall have mercy " (Proverbs 28: 13). We should carefully avoid the pathway of covering sin.

Another matter which is of great importance if we are to avoid mental tension, is that we should have some understanding of our make-up, and of the laws which govern the healthy functioning of our bodies and minds.

It is not necessary to go into technicalities as regards the nature of man, but there are two things in particular which I believe we need to recognise in relation to this whole question of mental tension.

The first is that our bodies, our minds and our spirits

(the spirit being the organ of God-consciousness), are very closely inter-related. We do all know in experience that our minds are affected by the condition of our bodies. When we are tired or sick, our minds are not as alert as when we are rested and well. When we are spiritually right our bodies are often quickened and helped and our minds renewed. Although man has different parts he is a unity, and should be considered as a unity. This simply means that if I want to avoid mental tension, and enjoy real mental health, I shall treat seriously the matter of physical health and spiritual health, I shall be prepared to discipline my body, and I will be careful of my ordinary and of my spiritual diet, so that I am feeding both body and soul on those foods which will be most conducive to physical and spiritual health.

The second thing which we need to recognise, is that we function on a pattern of alternating contraction and relaxation, or to put it more simply of alternating work and rest. Our muscles contract and relax; our hearts contract and relax about seventy times a minute; our stomachs work after a meal, and then need to rest a while before we eat again; our minds are capable of hard work which must then be followed by rest. God, Who made us, gave two laws to His people in the wilderness, which are based on this law of our make-up; those two laws are these: " Thou shalt work . . . thou shalt rest " (Exodus 34: 21). The principle behind those two laws has not altered, and yet numbers of Christians today are ignoring the second. When God gave that law, it was not concerning the rest of nightly sleep, it referred to the using of waking time for rest. I believe one of the reasons why Christians are increasingly subject to nervous and mental tension is because they will not take time for rest and relaxation. Christians who are interested in the prevention of mental tension should seek the Lord as regards His pattern for their lives in this matter of alternating work and rest. The details are an individual question for each one of us to work out with the Lord. I, personally, have found this thing to require real discipline and a real intention to find out the Lord's Will as it relates to my own life. A very important thing is to see that we are occupying our time with the things He wants us to do, and not taking upon ourselves things which He does not require of us. In times when it seems that there is far more to be done than is compatible with periods of relaxation, we can find that if we truly commit the matter to the Lord and refuse a sense of frustration, He shows us all sorts of little things that can be dropped, or else He sends help from most unexpected quarters, and so the burden is lightened and the pattern of work and rest can be obeyed.

Times of extra mental strain need to be followed by times of extra mental rest. Our minds have been given a marvellous power of recovery. It is possible for people to go through times of very great and prolonged mental and nervous strain, and yet to recover perfectly without any lasting tension, provided there is rest and relaxation to give the mind the chance to recover. If we want an example from Scripture of how God treated one who had been through great mental and spiritual strain we should read again the story of Elijah in 1 Kings 18 and 19, and learn from it.

It is not unspiritual to acknowledge that we are severely limited in what we can accomplish, and that we need our times of rest and relaxation. On the contrary it brings a child-like peace and simplicity to admit that we are indeed " frail children of dust and feeble as frail ". What a joy, too, to know that " He knoweth our frame, He remembereth that we are dust " (Psalm 103: 14).

We must now consider the prevention of tension which arises from the conflicts created by insecurity and lack of love in early childhood.   Unfortunately many of these do not come to the surface until tension is fully established and it is no longer a case of prevention but of treatment. It is, however, encouraging to know that there are many Christians whose childhoods have been insecure and unhappy, who have nevertheless been so transformed by the Lord and have so allowed His Spirit to straighten out their personalities, that they have never suffered from mental tension, and increasingly experience the joy and peace which He gives.   They have found a greater security than ever parents can give and a deeper and more wonderful love.

Perhaps the most important aspect of the subject of childhood insecurity for us to think about is the responsibility of Christian parents towards their children.   The responsibility to see that seeds of future mental tension are not sown.   Children need to be loved and to know that they are loved.   Each child needs to have its own special place in the hearts of its parents, and to know that it has that place.   Any favouritism of one child in a family at the expense of another, any preferential treatment produces conflict in the child mind.   I suppose this is so widely recognised that it is hardly necessary to mention it.   What is not so widely recognised is that a child's security depends not just on the love of the parents for the child, but upon the love of the parents for one another, and upon there being harmony between them.   We all know that separation or divorce shatters the security of the children concerned, but there is probably not such a clear understanding of the fact that any rift between parents, any lack of love and unity undermines the security of children. Unfortunately we must confess that as Christian parents we are often guilty in this respect.

This security produced by the mutual love of the parents and by the unity between them, is a wonderful picture of that security which we enjoy as children of God. That security is based not only on God's love for each one of His children, but upon the completely unchanging bond of love and unity which there is within the Godhead. This thought can be a great incentive to Christian parents to seek to do all in their power to maintain peaceful, loving relationships with one another. Notice the prayer of Jesus in John 17: 26, " That the love wherewith Thou hast loved Me may be in them."

Discipline is another essential in the production of security in children. Loving discipline, which is firm and just, creates security. Lack of discipline, through a wrong interpretation of love, or just through laziness, undermines the security of children. Discipline should not consist of threats which are never carried out, children should know that their parents mean what they say, and will do what they say. It is also necessary to understand something of the development of a child and the different kind of discipline necessary at different stages of its development. While a child is young it is right to demand unquestioning obedience, but as the adolescent years approach there must be a willingness to reason and give explanations. A helpful little book on this subject is Dr. Campbell Morgan's THE BIBLE AND THE CHILD.

Discipline should be matter-of-fact and not mixed up with emotional reactions in the parent. If a child is never punished in an outright, matter-of-fact way, but every time he does anything that displeases his parents he is punished by a heavy atmosphere of disapproval and hurt love, he will grow up, not controlled by a recognition of certain moral values, but with a dread of doing anything which will create the heavy atmosphere. This is very likely to show itself later in the fear associated with vague guilty feelings, which will arise whenever the young man or young woman does anything which he or she instinctively knows would be disapproved of by the parents. These guilty feelings are very difficult for young people to overcome and may produce real conflict.

When boys and girls reach adolescence, Christian parents always have the acute problem of what to allow them to do, and what is not to be allowed.   This problem needs much prayer, and wisdom beyond our own, but I think it is most important that parents should admit to their young people that the problem is one about which Christians differ, and then give reasons for having come to the particular decision made, at the same time admitting that they are not infallible and therefore may make mistakes, but that they are constantly prompted by a desire for the very best for their boys and girls.   To handle these matters with wisdom and love is very important and will have a part in helping young people later on to come to their own decisions unhampered by false feelings of guilt.

If young people are not to grow up with false guilty feelings concerning sex, Christian parents should seek the Lord's Face as to how and when to teach their children matters relating to sex, in the right way, and without embarrassment.

A great responsibility lies upon those of us who are parents !   We need to walk humbly with the Lord as we seek to prevent our children from later conflict and tension.   How thankful we should be for the Lord's overruling grace and mercy, which so frequently covers our blunderings and mistakes !

We saw that heredity plays a contributory part in some cases of mental tension and we must consider briefly how we can prevent these hereditary factors from gaining control in our lives. If we are conscious that we have inherited a tendency to mental tension or a temperament which is prone to such troubles as depression, it does not mean that we are necessarily less spiritual than others, but without being unduly introspective we should seek to understand ourselves and to face the particular type of temperament and nervous make-up which we have. In this way we can learn to be on our guard against inherited tendencies and to avoid things which may be dangerous for us. I was told by a man who had suffered serious attacks of depression that he had learnt that he must avoid taking part in controversy for this was a danger to him.

As we think of these things we do need to remember what a mighty Saviour we have. He is able to save us to the uttermost. As we seek unreservedly to commit ourselves to Him, we can find His power to unravel and control inherited traits as well as acquired ones.

If we are conscious of having been made of even frailer stuff than that of which the average frail human being is made, we need not despair, our God is a wonderful Potter, and He can make and has made some of His choicest vessels out of specially frail clay.

We have also thought about Satan's part in the causation of mental tension and so we must realise that it is important for us to know how we can resist his working. Paul said, concerning Satan, " We are not ignorant of his devices " (2 Corinthians 2: 11). We too should exercise ourselves to understand his devices, so that we may discern his activities and be on our guard. Let us remember again that he trades in lies, therefore we need constantly to depend upon the Holy Spirit's ministry that we may discern what is truth in all that is presented to our minds and reject what is not according to truth. This does not only apply to matters of doctrine, but to all our thoughts concerning ourselves, concerning other people, concerning our circumstances, and concerning the character and working of God Himself.

Perhaps one of the activities of Satan of which we most need to have knowledge is connected with his work as accuser of the brethren. Many of God's children are brought into conflict and mental distress through his accusations and through false feelings of guilt, and we need to know how to recognise these attacks and to face him when he hurls his accusations at us.

Let us remember that conviction from God and accusation from Satan are very different. God convicts so as to bring us to confession and restoration; Satan accuses so as to bring us to condemnation and despair. Satan seeks to produce in Christians the feeling that they must give up service for the Lord because of what they are like.

God's conviction through His Holy Spirit is quiet and definite, there is no doubt as regards the sin committed. Satan nags, and the one accused finds it difficult to discover whether he has or has not done wrong. God's dealings are with certainty and assurance, Satan's with uncertainty and doubt.

When a Christian recognises that Satan is accusing, and he is not sure whether the thing about which he is being accused is, in fact, right or wrong, he must know how to silence his accuser, otherwise the pain and conflict may continue for a long period of time and actually cause mental tension.

I would like to share what I have myself found, which has revolutionised my life as far as the severe conflict caused by this kind of accusation is concerned. It may sound very simple and child-like but it may help some other suffering child of God. I believe that Jesus, having died for me and taken up my cause before the Father, has

become my Advocate and I believe He gives me per-
mission to refer my cause to Him even as I would to a
human advocate. If I had an enemy who repeatedly
came to accuse me, I would put my case into the hands of
the best advocate I could find, and then whenever my
enemy would turn up to accuse me I would say, " I've
handed over my case to another, please go and talk to my
advocate, he'll answer for me." This is how I now face
Satan; whenever he starts to accuse, I say something like
this to him, " Satan, I have put my case into the hands of
Another, I really do not know whether I've done wrong or
not, but He knows; go and tell Him what you think. If
He knows I've done wrong He can tell me. I am not
dealing with you except through my Advocate." And
then I quietly get on with my work. I find that in the
majority of cases I never hear anything more about the
matter !

I discovered this way of treating Satan when studying
the Epistle to the Romans. As I filled my mind with the
teaching on justification, and then went on to read
Romans 8 over and over again, it seemed to me that a
suitable title for that chapter would be, " Out of the Law
Court and into the Father's House," and I saw that I
could leave the atmosphere and accusations of the Law
Court to my Advocate, the Lord Jesus Christ, Who would
represent me there, while I could sit at peace and rest in
the enjoyment of the Father's House !

Of course if we are suffering from Satan's accusations,
we must be careful to examine our hearts lest any unconfessed sin is being hidden, which is giving Satan a vantage
ground from which to attack us.

Another type of Satan's activity as the accuser, which
also brings people into real conflict, is that which is
based on a lie. For the prevention of tension in a case of

this kind it is necessary that the lie be exposed and the truth asserted. Perhaps the best way to make this clear is to give an example.

A young lady went through a very difficult experience, which, for several years, subjected her to great mental strain; she was very conscious of the strain, but did not have either a nervous or mental breakdown. Thirty years later she was subject to real torment and terrible fear, which most commonly gripped her if she woke in the night. She herself was quite definite that the fear and torment came from Satan. The specific fear was that she would have a mental breakdown, and she was frequently trying to guard herself from situations which she felt might be too much for her. Sometimes the mental conflict was so great that she wished she could have a complete breakdown so that she could escape from the torment. At all times she was quite convinced that she was much more likely to suffer from mental breakdown than the majority of people. On hearing the whole story it was quite evident that she was actually more stable mentally than a great many people, and in the many years that had passed there had been plenty of time for the mind to recover fully from the experience. It was suggested to her that in believing that she was more likely than most people to break down mentally, she was believing a lie about herself, and that she needed to affirm the truth, if she was to be free from the fear and torment to which she was subject. At first she did not accept this, but after three months of thought and prayer on the matter, she accepted that she had in fact been believing a lie, and agreed simply to affirm the truth when next Satan attacked her in this way. As far as I know, she has been completely free of this particular fear ever since. " Ye shall know the truth and the truth shall set you free."

CHAPTER 4

THE CURE OF TENSION

IS there a cure for tension ?   If so, how can a Christian
in a state of mental tension be cured ?   Is it enough to
take a course of tranquillizing drugs in the hope that the
relaxation they produce will, in itself, affect a cure ?
Will a change of occupation or perhaps a good holiday be
sufficient ?

These and other questions arise in the minds of those
who have discovered themselves to be suffering from
mental tension, or of those who long to help Christian
friends who are suffering in this way.

The first question, as to whether there is a cure for
tension can be answered easily and positively.   One who
is suffering from tension can be perfectly healed.   There
are many Christians who have suffered from varying
degrees and types of mental tension, who have found the
cure and are now enjoying mental and physical health.
The very fact that God promises His children peace and
rest of heart and mind must carry with it the assurance
that there is a way of passing from stress to rest.

Perhaps it is necessary to say a little more by way of
clarification.   We all know cases of tension who do not
seem to have been healed but that does not necessarily
mean that they *could* not have been healed.   Then there
are those who are healed but are very conscious that the
' scars remain ', and may also be more conscious of
weakness than they were before.   Maybe they are so

conscious of the scars and the weakness that they feel they have not really been healed, yet scars and weakness are not the same as active disease, and they can be used of God for His glory and to produce a greater dependence on Him. The positive and glorious fact is that God has given to His children His Holy Spirit, who is able to do a deep work of healing which reaches even to the sub-conscious depths of the personality. I have seen this demonstrated, and therefore I view every case with hope.

Real mental illness is right outside the scope of this little book, but as regards that, I simply have to accept that there are many cases which will never be healed in this life, just as I accept the same fact in many cases of physical deformities and some chronic physical illnesses. The problems which arise in the minds of some Christians regarding incurable cases is also outside the scope of this book.

The second question as to how that healing is brought about is not so easy to answer. Every case is different, every personality is different, and therefore details of treatment are bound to be different for each case. It is possible, however, to give some general principles which can be adapted to each individual case.

The condition itself is usually discovered in one of two ways. Either there are symptoms which lead to a visit to the doctor, who makes the diagnosis after careful examina-tion and consideration of the case; or else the one concerned begins to suspect that the cause of certain symptoms is mental tension. In the latter case it is always wise to go to the doctor for a thorough examination, remembering that symptoms which the patient thinks are due to mental tension may be discovered to have a physical basis.

The diagnosis of mental tension having been confirmed

and accepted, the first and most essential principle, if there is to be a cure, is that the case be fully and trustingly committed into the Hands of the Great Physician, the Lord Jesus Christ. There are several reasons why, in these cases, it is not sufficient for the Christian to rely primarily on the wisdom of his doctor or even on the best of Christian psychiatrists. One reason is that if there is to be a cure, the cause of the mental tension must be discovered. The psychiatrist, or doctor, or even the Christian friend, can do much to help uncover the underlying causes of tension, but it is the Lord alone Who fully knows us and Who is able to uncover our deepest problems, and Who alone can straighten out our personalities in a way so tender that no further harm is done to us in the process. He may use the psychiatrist or others less experienced, but in the final analysis it is He Who must do the work of restoring peace and order to the personality. Psalm 139 is a wonderful affirmation and prayer for any Christian suffering from mental tension. Hebrews 4: 12 and 13 also remind us of God's power to lay bare the depths of our personalities which are hidden to all human gaze.

Another reason why it is so essential to commit the case into the Hands of the Lord Jesus, is that in a special way Satan opposes the discovery of the cause, and the cure, of mental tension in a Christian. The Lord Jesus has won a full and final victory over Satan on the Cross, and He is experienced in bringing that victory into effect in the lives of His children. The Christian who is seeking to be cured from mental tension may expect a real battle with the powers of darkness, and needs to be in closest communication with the mighty Victor, the Lord Jesus Christ Himself.

The next principle in the cure of mental tension is, I

believe, a willingness to be healed.   Strangely enough, that is not always as easy as it sounds.   There is no doubt that fallen human nature is so deeply self-centred that there is a certain enjoyment in anything which draws attention to ourselves, even if it is only our own attention which is being drawn, and this may produce a peculiar reluctance to let go of our problems.

There is also a consciousness in the one suffering from tension, that the discovery of the cause may mean painful probing into things of which the sufferer is both afraid and ashamed, and for that reason there is an instinctive resistance to, rather than a willingness for, the healing process.   Are we not all ashamed of our Fears, our Frustrations, and our Resentments ? are we not naturally unwilling to have them exposed ?

Probably the greatest power to change any unwilling-ness to willingness, comes from the conviction that peace and rest of mind are God's will for the Christian.   God, in His grace, has given us the Holy Spirit, Whose whole desire is to bring about the will of God in our lives. Therefore, when God's will is revealed to a true Christian, there is that within him which responds with a willingness to have that will brought about, and which leads on to a quiet determination to enter into all God's promises.

The case having been handed over fully to the Lord, with a real willingness and desire for healing, the Christian who is suffering from mental tension must give the fullest co-operation to the Lord in the discovering of the basic cause of the tension.   It is possible for the Lord Himself to lay bare the conflict which is at the root of the trouble, without any human intervention.   In many cases He uses a human instrument, and in this He will guide the one who is genuinely desirous of being healed.   He may use a psychiatrist or a doctor (if Christian ones are available obviously you would choose them). He may use a minister, or some Christian friend with no special qualifications. Whether the patient is dealing directly with the Lord or with some human instrument he must be really honest. Here again we need to realise that shame instinctively hides, and it is difficult for one suffering from tension to be really honest with himself, with the Lord and with others. I have known someone suffering from mental tension to submit himself to several doctors and to a psychiatrist, and yet to keep hidden the one thing that really mattered.

In some cases healing follows the discovery of the cause without anything else being done. In other cases healing does not immediately follow, and in these cases the next principle is that the cause must be faced. Here again, particularly if the cause is fear, the instinctive reaction is to avoid facing the fear, and to do anything to manoeuvre circumstances so that the fear will not have to be faced. To face the cause and to continue facing it until it is overcome and healing is established, may take time and courage and persistent faith. In some cases the cause is so bound up with the patient's emotions that there needs to be much patient help given and much prayer, before deliverance comes.

All through this pathway which leads to cure there is need for patience. Patience with oneself and patient waiting upon God, with confidence that He is faithful and that He can and will give full restoration. There is also need for a continuous attitude of resistance to Satan, and of claiming from the Lord His victory over all Satan's wiles and lies.

Almost certainly at some stage in the treatment, the Christian suffering from mental tension will be advised to take tranquillizing drugs, or will be told that what he needs is a holiday or a change of environment. None of these things are wrong in themselves, and may give temporary relief, and help to produce a state of mind which is more capable of facing the real cause of the trouble, but they will not in themselves affect a cure.

Having been healed of mental tension, great care should be taken in the prevention of future tension, particularly in the specific sphere which caused the tension; this can be done along the lines suggested in the previous chapter.

Cases of mental tension are sufficiently common to make it probable that all of us who are Christians will meet such cases amongst fellow-Christians, and will desire to help in their cure. We may feel that lack of experience, or of a knowledge of psychology, makes us quite inadequate to take any part in helping another, but I believe that any Christian can be of great service to another who is suffering from mental tension, provided he or she will follow some simple principles. It is important that we should all be equipped to help others in this way, because there are many Christians suffering from various degrees of mental tension, who will never be able to consult a Christian psychiatrist or even a Christian doctor, and who greatly need the sympathetic help of a fellow-believer.

Let us think then of some of the principles which will help us to play a part in the cure of mental tension when we meet it in others.

First and foremost there is a need for a really sympathetic attitude towards the sufferer. Unfortunately, owing to misunderstanding of the condition, there is often a far from sympathetic attitude towards one who is suffering from tension. I have heard such expressions as, " His pain is just imagination," or in a rather scornful tone, " She's just neurotic." With these expressions we can unmeaningly be very cruel, for we are failing to realise that the symptoms of mental tension are not imaginary but real, in fact the distress of mental tension is usually greater than that associated with physical illness; and the pain, where pain is a symptom, is often more acute. We need to realise that the one suffering from mental tension is ill, and needs treating with even more sympathy than the one who is physically ill.

Even should the underlying cause of the tension be something which we consider to be the person's own fault we would do well to take heed to the description of a true priest, taken from among men, which is given in Hebrews 5: 2 " Who can have compassion on the ignorant, and on them that are out of the way; for that he himself also is compassed with infirmity ". A realisation that even those of us who are not suffering from tension, are yet, " compassed with infirmity ", will give us sympathetic and compassionate hearts towards those who are so affected.

In seeking to help in the cure of a case of tension, we must remember that we are dealing with two persons, not just one. We are dealing with the patient and with Satan. Satan strongly opposes the cure of mental tension in Christians, and we shall find ourselves in conflict with him as we put ourselves into the Lord's Hands to be instruments in such cures. Ephesians 6: 11-18 reminds us of the armour which we need to take if we are to gain the victory in this conflict, and of the fact that the place where the victory is gained is the place of prayer. We need to be constantly in prayer that Satan be defeated, that discernment is given, that the truth be brought to the light and that full cure be the result.

In many cases this all-important prayer ministry will be the only part which we can take in the cure. Added strength will be given to the prayer ministry if it is possible to join with one other in real agreed prayer, and as a result we shall see the Lord doing wonderful things according to His Promise in Matthew 18: 19, " If two of you shall agree on earth as touching any thing that they shall ask, it shall be done for them of My Father which is in heaven."

In some cases we may be called into personal dealings with the patient, and in this case we shall need the capacity to listen patiently and repeatedly, while we seek to uncover the basic cause of the condition. It is very seldom that the truth will come out in one talk, and we shall need to go away, and talk over all that has been said with the Lord, constantly casting ourselves upon Him, that His Spirit may give discernment and that we may be able to make a helpful and truthful contribution to the patient's own thinking. It is of vital importance that we do not impress our own opinion upon the patient, but that he himself comes to a clear, reasoned understanding of the cause of his trouble.

After the cause is found there is further need of prayer for, and with, the one who is seeking healing, that he may find the way of release. The patient needs much encouragement at this stage, and the one who is seeking to help will constantly need a wisdom beyond his own. That wisdom, God is always ready and willing to give to the one who asks Him for it. James 1: 5, " If any of you lack wisdom, let him ask of God, that giveth to all men liberally, and upbraideth not; and it shall be given him."

It is a wonderful privilege to have any share in helping one who is suffering from tension, and a tremendous joy to see release and rest of mind restored to one of God's children. In this particular ministry, if it is ever given to us, we are absolutely dependent on the power and leading of the Holy Spirit. It is also a great encouragement to realise that, because the Holy Spirit is the One Who can pierce to the very depths of the human personality, and bring to the light, and to the memory, things hidden and forgotten, a humble Christian filled with the Spirit and absolutely dependent on the Spirit, may be used to bring healing to a suffering fellow-Christian, in spite of very little knowledge of medicine or psychology.

I think a special warning needs to be given to those who are seeking to help others. We need to recognise signs or symptoms of real mental and emotional illness and of physical illness so that we do not continue to try to help one who really needs to be passed on to an expert. To recognise physical illness is not very difficult, and I have already said that if there are any physical symptoms a doctor should be consulted. There are certain things which point to real mental or emotional illness and it would be wise to bear these in mind. The most important are delusions (abnormalities of thought, e.g. the man who thinks he is the king of England, or the man who thinks that all his friends are spying on him), hallucinations (seeing things that are not there), any suicidal tendency (even the threat of doing it), violence, deep or long lasting depression and what is called escapism (e.g. the patient who, when pressure of circumstances become too great, goes to sleep at any time or in any place !). Any one suffering from any of these things should be passed on to a doctor at once, who will in all probability pass the patient on to a specialist.

CHAPTER 5

"BUT IF NOT . . ."

WHEN Shadrach, Meshach and Abed-nego were threatened with the burning fiery furnace if they did not bow down and worship the image which Nebuchadnezzar had set up, they said, " Our God Whom we serve is able to deliver us from the burning fiery furnace, and he will deliver us out of thine hand, O king.   BUT IF NOT, . . . be it known unto thee, O king, that we will not serve thy gods, nor worship the golden image which thou hast set up."   (Daniel 3: 17, 18.)

The previous chapters have been written in the hope that they may be used to prevent what is known as " nervous or mental breakdown ", in which the patient becomes temporarily unable to cope with the ordinary demands of life and work.   But for the sake of Christians who may read this book during a breakdown or after it, I am adding this chapter.   One reason for doing so is that if you are passing through the experience of any sort of a breakdown, or if you are struggling to recover, what has already been said *may* simply bring you into a deeper state of guilt, condemnation and despair.

So let us think together briefly about that ' BUT IF NOT '.   Suppose you have not been delivered, suppose the breakdown has come, suppose the dark waters have closed over your head, what then ?

One important thing to remember is that not all ' breakdowns ' are due to unrelieved tension.   Specialists are not able to state the cause dogmatically, there are often several factors; and your illness is not necessarily the result of the tension which we have been considering. To realise this may be the means of saving you from much self-condemnation and feelings of guilt.

There are several things which we can learn from this story of the burning fiery furnace, even though the experience of the fire came as the result of different circumstances. Firstly, there was the Presence of the Son of God with them in the fire. You may be quite unconscious of His Presence, in fact you will probably feel that He has forsaken you and turned His back upon you, and it will bring you no comfort to be told that He is with you. Nevertheless, the fact remains, and others looking into the fire from outside may see that He is there. His Presence means that He will not allow the fire to do you permanent harm, He will have it all under His control, and one day you will know that He was doing for you what He did for those three men, loosing their bonds. *They* went into the fire bound, they came out free. God will one day bring *you* out into a place of freedom, and you will realise that He has been at work in the fire, and in the darkness, doing in your personality that which could have been accomplished in no other way.

Next, notice that the fire failed to change the intention of the three men. They kept steadfast in will, that they would not serve Satan and would not deny God. It is possible to maintain a like intention even when stripped of all pleasurable " feelings ". The fire we are speaking of nearly always strips away feelings, except those of guilt and suffering. We little realise how we depend on " feelings " until they have gone. Yet even when the darkness is very deep, there can be maintained an intention to obey God and to be faithful, as far as possible, to Him. I think this is what matters to God. In "Screwtape Letters" C. S. Lewis makes Screwtape say, when writing about the troughs of human experience, "Do not be deceived, Wormwood. Our cause is never more in danger than when a human, no longer desiring, but still intending, to do our Enemy's will, looks round upon a universe from which every trace of Him seems to have vanished, and asks why he has been forsaken, and still obeys." Of course it is possible for even the will to be broken down through excessive physical or mental torture. We have all heard of cases where Christians who have been persecuted, have given way under physical torment or the mental anguish of brain-washing and have denied the Lord. What a comfort it is to know that the Lord knows and understands how much pressure we can bear, and in many cases He has given another chance to confess Him. The story of Archbishop Cranmer, who recanted but afterwards repented, and died bravely as a martyr is a case in point. But if you know that in spite of breakdown and mental suffering, there has been deep within you the intention that you will not change your allegiance from God to Satan, this knowledge can lead you to see that the very thing which you thought was showing that you were not a Christian, is in fact revealing that you are; for you could not have maintained that intention apart from the work of God within your soul.

Satan may take advantage of your being stripped of all pleasurable "feeling" to bring deep doubts concerning the reality of your conversion and the forgiveness of your sins. The assurance of your salvation is lost, and you are flooded with the remembrance of past sins; and now your "feelings" of guilt and of being forsaken seem to prove to you that you are not forgiven, that you are not God's child. If this happens, you must go back to the faith-

fulness of God and the Word of God. The Word of Jesus
stands for ever, " Him that cometh to Me I will *in no wise*
cast out " (John 6: 37). If you came to Him, and
received Him as your Saviour, He will never give you up
whatever you may feel and whatever you have done.
You can face Satan with the Word of God and assert, in
spite of all your feelings, or lack of feelings, that

" The soul that on Jesus hath leaned for repose,
He will not, He will not, desert to its foes;
That soul, though all hell should endeavour to shake,
He'll never, no, never, no, never forsake."

You can also *act*, as far as is possible, as a child of God,
whatever your feelings. This particularly applies to
convalescence when you can attend church services, and
read your Bible and pray even if it all seems automatic and
unreal. It is through these channels that God will again
reveal Himself.

There is one more thing about the fire which I would
like to mention, and that is that it did not last for ever,
there came the moment when the three men stepped out of
the peculiar and unfamiliar circumstances of the fire into
the ordinary surroundings of life. Your fire will not last
for ever. There will come the day when the darkness will
pass and light dawn, when the song of praise will once
again well up in your heart and the circumstances of life
will become normal. It may seem a very long time, but
as you look back, you will see something of what God was
doing, and it may be that through it He will give you a
message that can be used to help others.

Maybe you are not going through such an experience
of " breakdown " or illness yourself but are closely
associated with someone who is, and you long to be able to
help but do not know how. Be very patient. Pray
much, especially that Satan may not get an advantage and

hinder what God is doing. Do not alter in your attitude towards your friend. This may speak to him or her of the unchanging rock-like character of our God. Be compassionate, remember Job's cry to his friends, " Have pity upon me, have pity upon me, O ye my friends; for the hand of God hath touched me " (Job 19: 21). Stand by prayerfully in case the Lord shows you something which you can say or do to help. Remember that the fire will not last for ever, and you will yet be given the joy of seeing your friend delivered and joining you in praising God for what He has done.

You may say, " But I know a Christian who never did come out of this fire in this life, death came before deliverance and healing were given." It is still true to say that for a child of God the fire never lasts for ever. Suppose what you think to be the worst happens and death comes before deliverance ? Suppose the darkness never lifts in this life ? Is not death deliverance ? Is it not the beginning of light that will never fade ? And will not the fire and the valley of the shadow, when for ever past, seem short compared with the eternal glory ? " Our light affliction which is for the moment, worketh for us more and more exceedingly an eternal weight of glory." (2 Corinthians 4: 17, R.V.)

We may not understand God's way, but we can trust our Father, and when we get Home, He will explain all.

CHAPTER 6

THE POSITIVE CHARACTERISTICS OF A MIND AT EASE

THERE are many verses and passages in the Bible which reveal to us some of the characteristics of a mind at ease; of these, perhaps the most helpful to consider is Matthew 11: 28, 29. These well-known verses record for us the gracious invitation of the Lord Jesus, " Come unto Me, all ye that labour and are heavy laden, and I will give you rest. Take My yoke upon you and learn of Me; for I am meek and lowly in heart: and ye shall find rest unto your souls."

We have here two kinds of rest; a rest which is *given* to those who come to Jesus, and a rest which is *found* by those who take His yoke upon them, and learn of Him. I believe the first particularly refers to rest from the basic heart burdens which human beings carry because of sin and estrangement from God, and the second to that rest of heart and mind which is found by those who, having come to Jesus, go on to a life of submission to Him and learning of Him.

There may be one reading this book who is battling with inner conflict and tension and who has not yet taken the first step of coming to Jesus and receiving Him as Saviour and Lord, and so I would like to spend a little time in considering that first part of the Lord's wonderful invitation.

In the Bible we find a number of basic heart burdens mentioned, from which Jesus gives us rest when we come to Him. These are all burdens which cause disruption and conflict in the personality.

The first basic heart burden is that of sin. In Psalm 38: 4 we read, " For mine iniquities have gone over mine head: as an heavy burden they are too heavy for me." Many are not even conscious of that burden, yet all the time it is there doing its disruptive work in the depths of their beings. From the beginning the essence of sin has been rebellion against God. Rebellion against its Maker cannot bring peace and rest to the personality. It is only by coming to Jesus that rest can be found from this burden of sin and rebellion. One of the most beautiful descriptions of the way man finds rest from this burden has been given to us in the PILGRIM'S PROGRESS. John Bunyan describes Christian as carrying a heavy burden from which he constantly sought rest. Then came a time in Christian's journey when, John Bunyan tells us, " he came at a place somewhat ascending, and upon that place stood a cross, and a little below, in the bottom, a sepulchre. So I saw in my dream, that just as Christian came up with the cross, his burden loosed from off his shoulders, and fell from off his back, and began to tumble, and so continued to do till it came to the mouth of the sepulchre, where it fell in, and I saw it no more. Then was Christian glad and lightsome, and said with a merry heart, He hath given me rest by His sorrow, and life by His death. Then he stood awhile to look and wonder; for it was very surprising to him that the sight of the cross should thus ease him of his burden. . . . Then Christian gave three leaps of joy, and went on singing,

> Thus far did I come laden with my sin;
> Nor could aught ease the grief that I was in,
> Till I came hither: what a place is this !
> Must here be the beginning of my bliss ?

Must here the burden fall from off my back ?
Must here the strings that bound it to me crack ?
Blessed cross ! blessed sepulchre ! blessed rather be
The man that there was put to shame for me ! "

It is because Jesus carried our burden of sin when He died upon the Cross, that He can give us rest from that burden when we come to Him.

Job knew another basic heart burden. We read in Job 7: 20, " I am a burden to myself." Of course the burden of self and the burden of sin are really parts of the same burden, but there are many people who do not realise that they are burdened with sin, who yet do realise that they are carrying a burden of self. In my own experience, it was the knowledge that I was entirely self-centred, and that I could get no rest from myself, which caused me to come to Jesus. Our personalities were not made to be self-centred, they were made to be God-centred; it is sin that has made us wrongly centred, and this self-centredness causes friction and conflict within us. There is only one way of receiving rest from this burden, it is to come to Jesus, Who took our old self-centred nature to the Cross and Who can change us by His resurrection life lived in us by His Spirit, into being Christ-centred, so that we can say with Paul, " I am crucified with Christ, nevertheless I live, yet not I, but Christ liveth in me " (Galatians 2: 20).

There is only one other burden which I would like to mention here, and that is the burden of outward religious observance without inward spiritual life, which Jesus Himself denounced in speaking of the Scribes and Pharisees. " They bind heavy burdens and grievous to be borne, and lay them on men's shoulders; but they themselves will not move them with one of their fingers " (Matthew 23: 4). I believe there are many people

today, suffering from conflict and tension, who are seeking
to find a cure in outward religious observances, when they
have not yet received inward spiritual life. They are
seeking by good works, by Church-going, by Bible-read-
ing, by prayer, by kindness, and such things, to please God
in the hope that He will relieve them of their conflict and
tension. In actual fact they discover that these things
simply add to their burdens rather than bringing rest.
Hebrews 4: 10 tells us that " he that is entered into his
rest, he also hath ceased from his own works ". There is a
wonderful rest which Jesus gives to those who will drop
all their efforts and come to Him in simple trust, believing
that all that is necessary for salvation (the meaning of
which includes being made whole), was done by Him
when He lived, died, rose again, ascended to heaven, and
sent to us the gift of His Holy Spirit.

> " Weary, working, burdened one,
> Wherefore toil you so ?
> Cease your doing; all was done
> Long, long ago."

If we will come to Him, His own promise stands for ever
sure, " Him that cometh to Me I will in no wise cast out "
(John 6: 37).

Many young Christians become discouraged because
they expect that, having come to the Lord Jesus, and
having received this rest from basic heart burdens, they
will know a lasting rest of mind and an end of conflict,
and they find that this is not the case. For such, the
second part of the Lord's invitation is what is needed for
consideration and response. There is still a rest of the
whole personality which can only be found by taking His
yoke and by learning of Him.

To be under the yoke in Bible times meant to be in
submission. Not only coming to Jesus Christ but real

submission to Him is necessary if we are to find rest. There may be a definite transaction, when we submit ourselves fully to His rule. After that, we shall find that He works our submission out in our lives by opening up to us fresh areas in our personalities, in which we find that there is still conflict and rebellion. As He does that, and as we yield more and more of these areas in submission to Him, we find increasing rest. It is written of Him " of the increase of His government and peace there shall be no end ".

> " And as Thy kingdom doth increase,
>   So shall Thine ever-deepening peace."

The yoke also speaks of service. The ox in the yoke is a picture of patient, steady, God-appointed labour. One characteristic of a mind at ease, is that it is a mind which is at rest in the midst of hard work and service for the Lord; it is a mind which is at rest because it has a God-appointed service to carry out. The Lord Jesus has a specific yoke for each one who belongs to Him; it may be in what is commonly known as Christian service, it may be in the humblest ordinary job; it may be in the Mission Field, it may be in an office, it may be in a home. Wherever it is, whatever it is, if it is known to be His yoke and accepted as such, it will bring rest.

> " Peace, perfect peace, by thronging duties press'd ?
>   To do the will of Jesus, this is rest."

The Lord Jesus also tells us that we are to learn of Him if we would find rest to our souls. We never get beyond the need for learning from Him. Who teacheth like Him ? What rest it brings to learn from Him, and yet how reluctant we often are to learn. I have found the Lord changing my prayer concerning lack of peace of mind, since I really thought about this invitation of the

Lord Jesus. I used always to cry to the Lord for deliverance if I found I had lost my peace and rest, and plead with Him to give me a mind at ease. I now ask Him to teach me why I have become upset, why there is conflict when there should be peace. I then find that He teaches me what is the underlying cause of the unrest, and I can put that right. A willingness to learn is an outstanding characteristic of a mind at ease.

The Lord Jesus gave us a reason as to why we are to take His yoke upon us and learn of Him. That reason is that He is meek and lowly in heart. I think that this indicates that two great characteristics of a mind at ease are meekness and lowliness. The Lord Jesus, when He walked this earth as the Son of Man, was subjected to all kinds of stress and strain, yet He never showed the slightest sign of abnormal mental tension. He suffered pressure from foes, pressure from friends, pressure from circumstances, pressure from Satan, physical, mental, and spiritual pressure; and yet through it all He had such peace that when we read His Words, " Peace I leave with you, My peace I give unto you," our hearts know that that is the very kind of peace we want, *His* peace, which He displayed in the midst of all those pressures, when here on earth. Is He then telling us that the two characteristics of His wonderful personality which in particular made it possible for Him to have a mind at ease, are meekness and lowliness ? I think He is.

Let us think of those two characteristics.

Years ago I heard a godly minister say that in the meaning of the Greek word for meekness there is the thought of an animal being broken in. I have never forgotten that, but I have never found it written down until recently I read the following concerning the meaning of the Greek word ' *praus* ' which is translated ' meek ':

" That brings us to the use of ' *praus* ' which really illumines the whole matter. In Greek ' *praus* ' is used in one special sense. It is used—as is ' *mitis* ' in Latin—for a beast which has been tamed. A horse which was once wild but has become obedient to the bit and to the bridle is ' *praus* '."[1] So we can safely say that to be meek is to be broken in. Think of the young colt kicking and resisting the master's controlling hand. Think of the ox when it is first put into the yoke, utterly rebellious, doing everything in its power to break free. Then think of the same colt or the same ox, quiet, submissive, responding to every direction that its master gives; gentle and subdued so that its reaction to its master or to others need never be feared. What a picture of the meekness of Jesus. Not one trace of rebellion in Him, He came down from heaven to do the will of His Father not His own will (John 6: 38). All through His life He was utterly submissive to the directions of His Father, until at the end His very death and resurrection were in obedience to the Father's command, " I have power to lay it (My life) down, and I have power to take it again. This commandment have I received of My Father " (John 10: 18).

Not only was Jesus utterly submissive to the Father, but He was gentle (which is another meaning of ' praus ') towards others. Never did He answer back when provoked, never was He resentful or bitter, the depths of that gentleness were revealed when, as they nailed Him to the Cross, He prayed, " Father, forgive them for they know not what they do."

In Isaiah 50: 5, 6 we have a description of the meekness of Jesus, " The Lord God hath opened mine ear, and I was not rebellious, neither turned away back. I gave my back to the smiters, and my cheeks to them that plucked off the hair: I hid not my face from shame and spitting."

The word translated "lowly" is in other places translated "humble". The second characteristic which is so wonderfully displayed in the life of the Lord Jesus is His humility. In Philippians 2: 3-8 Paul tells us to have this same characteristic of mind that Jesus had, and he then tells us the two great marks of humility in the Lord Jesus. The first we find in verse 7, "He took upon Him the form of a servant".

In Luke 22: 27 we read the words of the Lord Himself, "I am among you as he that serveth". His humility was shown by His willingness to serve others, even to washing the disciples' feet, a task usually left to the lowest slave. The second mark of humility which Paul mentions is that "He humbled Himself, and became obedient unto death, even the death of the Cross" (verse 8).

Here then are the characteristics which we must learn of the Lord Jesus if we would find rest, if we would enjoy a mind at ease. Meekness from which all rebellion has been stripped, which is utterly submissive to God's Will, accepting quietly everything which He brings into the life, and which shows itself in gentleness towards others; not resentful or unforgiving of any treatment received at the hands of others; and lowliness or humility, which shows itself in willingness to be a servant of all, and which submits to death, even the death of the cross.

Because that last point is so important in the finding of a mind at ease, and because nature is so deeply self-centred, I would like to say a little more about it. When Jesus died on the Cross He not only carried our sins, He carried our sinful human nature, and in His death made an end of the dominion and rule of that nature. He was then buried and rose from the dead into newness of life, which life He shares with us by His Holy Spirit. Because of His death He gives us the right to claim the breaking of the dominion and rule of the old sinful human nature, the self life, and He asks us to be obedient to that death, as He was. For us, that means a willingness for the end of the rule of self or the old sinful human nature, and as we bow to that death of self, there is, manifested within us by His Spirit, the risen life of the Lord Jesus. We are then called upon to take up our cross daily, as the Lord Jesus puts it, submitting in every detail of our lives to the death of self that the life of Jesus may be manifested in our mortal bodies. 2 Corinthians 4: 10, 11. It is this life of Jesus Himself, set free within us by the humility which is obedient unto death, even the death of the cross, which brings His rest and His peace into our whole personalities.

Let me in closing, draw a brief word sketch of the one who is increasingly finding rest, and therefore enjoying a mind at ease. He or she is one who has come to Jesus with the burdens of sin and self and outward religious observances, and has left them at the Cross, receiving from Him the rest which He gives. He or she is one who is increasingly submitting to the dominion of Jesus, and to the service of Jesus; who is constantly willing and seeking to learn of Jesus, and who in particular is learning to allow His meekness and lowliness to manifest themselves in all the circumstances of life.

To such an one the promise is sure, " Ye shall find rest unto your souls."

(¹) A NEW TESTAMENT WORDBOOK by William Barclay.

Other verses and passages which are helpful in contributing to a mind at ease:

Proverbs 17: 22 with Philippians 4: 4   Matthew 6: 24-34.
Psalms 37; 42; 46; 62; 77.   Philippians 4: 6, 7.
Isaiah 26: 3, 4; 40: 28-31.

THE BLESSED SECRET

" ' Be all at rest, my soul ! '   Oh ! blessed secret
   Of the true life that glorifies thy Lord;
   Not always doth the busiest soul best serve Him,
   But he who resteth on His faithful word.

' Be all at rest ! ' for rest is highest service;
   To the still heart God doth His secrets tell;
   Thus shalt thou learn to wait, and watch, and labour,
   Strengthened to bear, since Christ in thee doth dwell.

' Be all at rest ! ' for rest alone becometh
   The soul that casts on Him its every care;
' Be all at rest ! ' so shall thy life proclaim Him
   A God who worketh and who heareth prayer.

' Be all at rest ! ' so shall thou be an answer
   To those who question, ' Who is God, and where ? '
   For God is rest, and where He dwells is stillness,
   And they who dwell in Him that rest shall share."

FREDA HANBURY ALLEN.